THE GOD OF ALL POWER

Encountering God and Raising the Dead

Prophet Sam Vardhan

Edited by: Sara Shallenberger

All scriptures are from the New King James Version of the Bible unless otherwise indicated.

ISBN: 979-8-9866295-0-6 (paperback)

ISBN: 979-8-9866295-1-3 (eBook)

KDP ISBN: 9798353973416

- - - - - - - - - - - - - - - -

Permission: For information on getting permission for re-
prints and excerpts, contact:

Parenting Connections Publishing Group 2001 Timberloch
Place, Suite 500

The Woodlands, TX 77380

info@parentingconnections.net

I am not ashamed of the gospel, for it is the power of God unto salvation, for the Jew first and then the Gentile.

Romans 1:16

My message and my preaching were not with persuasive words of wisdom, but with a demonstration of the Spirit's power.

1 Cor. 2:14

"I tell you the truth, anyone who believes in me will do the same works I have done, and even greater works, because I am going to be with the Father.

John 14:12

Now to him who is able to do immeasurably more than all we ask or imagine, according to his power that is at work within us, to him be glory in the church and in Christ Jesus throughout all generations, for ever and ever! Amen.

Eph. 3:20-21

CONTENTS

FORWARD

A s the earth moves closer to the return of its Creator, The Father of Lights is preparing His Son's bride for the great Wedding Feast. The preparation of the Church is perfected through the ministry given to men and women called by the Lord and Anointed by His Spirit. As a minister of the Gospel of Jesus Christ, I believe that the United States of America and Nations of the world will begin to see great revivals and souls crying out for Salvation. The Lord is beginning to redeem Time back from darkness into the light of His dear Son, through the formation of Prophetic Ministers!

The Church is hungry for unity among believers of every nation, tribe, and tongue.

Prophet Sam V. has been called by the Spirit of the Lord for this time and season to see the harvest come in for the Glory of God!

Prophet Sam has both the Gifting of the Spirit and the grace to minister unto many cultures and followers of Christ!

As you read this powerful book you will yearn to see the Spirit of God move in your life and family. His encounter with the Lord as well as how his family played such a vital role in his Faith, helps us to understand God's desire is for the Supernatural to become part of our everyday lives.

As the Holy Spirit personally reveals that He is Anointing David's to replace the spirit of Saul in the Church, I expect to see the ministry of Prophet Sam go into all the world to prepare the Bride for His Coming.

Pastor Ram Tovar

Galveston, Texas, USA

INTRODUCTION

Some people in our lives are not only divine appointments but are also great gifts from Jesus to us. Samuel Vardhan is one of these people.

Prophet Samuel Vardhan has a powerful calling of the Lord to reach the lost and prepare the body of Christ for these last days before His return. He has a deep understanding of the things of God, wisdom and maturity beyond his years and a passion for being used by the Lord to see people saved, healed, and set free. Prophet Samual has a supernatural hunger to see the gospel demonstrated with power and to see God do what He has always done, open the eyes of the blind, the ears of the deaf, make the lame walk, preach the gospel to the poor and raise the dead.

This book might be your first introduction to the ministry of Prophet Samuel. His ministry is marked by a true passion for accuracy and detail in prophecy. His humble and submissive heart is like a magnet for the Holy Spirit to flow through him with accurate words about peoples' hearts, callings, finances, relationships, names and details that only a person walking in the office of prophet would be able to access.

But as spectacular as his prophetic anointing, and as impressive his record for dead raising truly is, his most outstanding character trait is His deep love for Jesus and humility and kindness towards people.

Prophet Samuel carries a deep kindness and genuine caring for people that was developed out of seasons of suffering and his encounters with the Lord. He has a beautiful heart for the body of Christ, and a deep evangelical heart to see both the beggar on the street and the masses saved.

Sitting down with Prophet Samuel to record his call to ministry and quest to see the dead raised was an honor and deep joy. Our first part of the conversation revolved around 'in India we don't count a person raised from the dead who was on life support' and went forward from there!

As Samuel recounted firsthand his experiences in the Lord, the Holy Spirit would fall in the room and minister the tangible Presence and Glory of the Lord Jesus. It is my prayer that as you sit and read these pages, the same anointing that God poured out during the writing of this book, He pours out into your heart and room as you read it.

Above anything else that this book is or represents, this book is a testimony of Jesus. It is indeed 'HIs Book' and 'His Story' which showcases the reality of God's power and desire to do the same works through our lives as He did through His own Son Jesus. And even greater.

There is a real strategy room in heaven. It is a place the Lord allowed me to encounter as a child where the angelic meet to discuss their role 'behind the scenes' on earth to ensure God's purposes are accomplished in our lives. It is in this realm that the Lord sees your life and mine. He orchestrates times, and seasons, people and purposes for His kingdom and His glory. It is both our personal honor to have connected with Prophet Samuel, one of the details orchestrated from that heavenly realm, and our joy to play a role in connecting this heavenly realm with you.

Many blessings to you as you read and discover the Lord, who knew you before you were in your mother's womb. Just like the Lord said He had 'great plans' and 'big plans' for Prophet Samuel, He has them for you as well! Anything you can see in the Word, you have His Personal permission to believe Him to see Him do in your life as well.

I am honored to know prophet Samuel Vardhan, and pleased to have the opportunity to share his story and his ministry with you.

Keep pursuing Jesus, there is much more that lays ahead of us than lays behind us.

In Christ, Sara Shallenberger

H2:2 Ministries

Author of "The Strategy Room of God"

Galveston, Texas USA

CHAPTER 1:

MY STORY BEGINS

My story really begins with my grandmother Lingamah. My mother and father already had one son and one daughter and were happy and content with their family of four! Our family was a Middle class like many Indian families, close-knit, with my grandmother living in our home. There was never a time my grandmother was not part of my family's daily life.

During the day, my father worked on the railways and my mother spent her days tending to our home and raising the children. Our home was filled with the bright colors and fragrant smells of curry, cloves and turmeric. I can recall pictures on our walls were adorned with the gods that were to bless, protect and bring us good fortune and success. We had daily evening Hindu prayer, in our little prayer or puja room.

So, this was our family, which was happy and lively. But in the eyes of my grandmother, there was something not quite right!

My grandmother wanted my parents to have one more child! In the way that only a grandmother can, she exercised the 'power of a grandmother to influence' and relentlessly and rather unashamedly told them that she needed one more grandchild. As she was a woman of prayer, already following the Christian faith, I am not sure my parents ever really had a chance resisting her! Not only was my grandmother praying over our family every night, but unbeknownst to my parents at the time, she was actively petitioning the Lord to send her 'one more grandchild' who would be a 'mighty man of God.' It was a specific request. It was a bold request. And this little Indian grandmother was not going to give my parents any rest until they agreed with her and agreed to have one more grandchild!

The evidence of my grandmother's great faith and prayer life is that the day came when I was born! It was December 11, 1993, in Kazipet, Telangana India!

My parents not only were blessed with their third child, but my grandmother specifically got a grandson, whom she had already determined would be a man of God. It turns out that my grandmother's prayers had gone out so far ahead of my arrival, that as I was born, the nurse who delivered me held me up to the Lord and dedicated me to a life of serving Jesus.

But all of this had happened in my life long before I had any knowledge of what had been prayed over my life and long before I knew there was a God who had ordained me and called me and who designed me to carry great destiny in Him.

As far as I knew growing up, I was going to grow up in a typical way and felt no great pull toward God or the supernatural things of God. My father and mother had both been raised Hindu and raised their children in the same manner. Not only did we have our evening time of prayer, but my father was a very gifted singer and sang often in our community temple. I watched my parents give evening offerings in our prayer room and happily played with brother and sister in our home with pictures of the Hindu gods looking over us. I enjoyed our religious traditions and learned a lifestyle of asking the gods to protect and bless me. Our home was filled with activity, and often filled with our neighbors, as my mother was a very good cook and either invited them to our home or sent food to them.

My parents were a very happy couple and as normal in many Indian families, our extended family was large.

My father had five sisters who each had many children of their own. He spent his years trying to help each of their families and in the process our family became broke and started to amass debt. That left my father to work hard and work long hours in order to be the best support he could to our family.

Because of his dedication and exemplary work ethic, all of us children were expected to study hard in school and focus our attention and efforts into becoming attorneys, doctors, or engineers. We watched my father leave early in the morning, commute to work and arrive late at night, sometimes after we had gone to bed. It developed a strong desire in myself and my siblings to do our best and make our parents proud of us. We each grew up wanting to be the biggest blessing to our family that we could.

Within this context, I grew up knowing the expectation my parents carried for me and understanding the importance that excelling in school would have in helping to improve our family situation. The better I did at school, the better university I could be accepted into, and the better job and income prospects I would have.

But the truth of the matter was, I did not care much for school! I was careful to study and stay far out of the reach of my parent's disapproval, but I did not enjoy sitting in class, laboring over books, and peering into the finer aspects of math, history, language, and grammar! No, I preferred to be outside playing! I felt it was a much better lifestyle to move and be a boy of action and adventure than be confined to a desk in the four walls of the schoolhouse. My mother, observing I was happier moving than sitting, quickly found some tasks to assign to me that would capitalize on my excess of energy.

In my mother's generosity, she would cook pans and pots filled with Indian flatbread pastry and coconut water, a couple of desserts and lemon rice, wrap them in a cloth and send me as a courier delivering the hot food to our neighbors. I was the youngest and this task suited me well! I enjoyed the interactions with my neighbors and delivering much welcomed food started to develop in me, a heart for service and that I indeed was my neighbor's keeper. These were happy days and wonderful days, that the Lord was already using to work within me a heart of compassion and interest in others, long before I had any firsthand knowledge of Him.

Just like my Grandmother was instrumental in my parents having me as their third child, she also played an important role in my family coming to Christ. My grandmother was the first Christian in our family. Before I was born, she had become very ill and wrote a letter to the well-known Indian evangelist, D G S Dhinakaran, believing that God would heal her. When the man of God wrote back to her by post card, she was healed. My grandmother was very thankful and gave God the glory for healing her. My family, not Christians at the time, were very happy but very surprised. It didn't make much sense to them that a foreign God would have any power to or interest in healing someone in their family! My family was pleased but had no real reason to leave their current belief system. So instead of my entire family turning to the Lord after seeing this miracle, the Lord had another plan to draw us each into salvation.

After my grandmother Lingamah was healed, my family was amazed enough that he had no reason to oppose any of her Christian activities. But as for him, he continued to be active in the Hindu temple, singing and enjoying the Hindu way of life. But that was only going to last for a few years, for God had greater and grand plans in store for my life as well as my whole family.

SALVATION IS FOR YOU AND FOR YOUR ENTIRE HOUSEHOLD

"Believe on the Lord Jesus, and you will be saved— you and your household." Acts 16:31

Because my grandmother had been supernaturally healed by the power of God, and loved Jesus, of course she wanted the rest of her family to come to salvation. Remember, in fact, that her sole purpose in cajoling my parents to have a third child, was that she wanted a preacher or man of God in the family! So, while my parents continued being active in their faith, my grandmother also stayed active living out her faith, bringing the people of God around our family every opportunity she could. You might say that my grandmother was the first on-the-ground evangelist I ever knew!

As is custom in India, my grandmother lived with our family, sharing the same home, kitchen, and mealtimes with us. Every evening she would spend time in prayer, praying over my parents and my siblings and me. She would pray and ask the Lord to save each one of us, reminding Him of His promise that salvation was for her and for her ENTIRE household. As she grew older every year, she was determined to see the Lord save our household while we were still young children and would have the opportunity to hear His call on our lives and decide to serve Him in our youth.

She did not want her family to be separated from her in eternity, and more than that, wanted her grandchildren to be mighty in the Lord and used in His last days harvest in India. This was very important to her. She had lived a full life in India and seen the darkness that lay over much of the population and wanted the light of the gospel to shine bright and bring many to salvation.

My grandmother loved the Christian fellowship in our village and invited many pastors to our home for meals. She had a tremendous love for those who labored in the work of the gospel and proclaimed the good news about the power of God to save and heal. My father loved our family and loved the joyful peace that rested in our home. He never had any issue with people of other faiths, and so when these pastors would come to eat, my mother would graciously cook and prepare the meal.

My parents loved people. All kinds of people.

They were very community minded and believed in sharing hospitality and honoring guests in our home, even if they were serving in a religion that was different from theirs. I was young, and didn't have any great pull for God. Despite my grandmother's prayers, I was content to run and have adventures outside with my siblings and friends. I was more interested in action and adventure than in a God that I could not see with my eyes.

One night my grandmother wanted to attend a Christian meeting in our area, and so asked my older brother to take her. The meeting was not too far from our home and was being held by Man of GOD Judson Abraham, a well-known spirit empowered evangelist in India. My brother agreed, and really had just planned on dropping my grandmother off and then leaving. That, however, was not the Lord's plan for that evening.

The Bible says that every one of our days is written in a book before one of them came to be. Psalm 139:16. My grandmother had been standing on Acts 16:31. Judson Abraham had been believing for many souls to be won in India, and the Lord had already orchestrated a day and time when all of these prayers of the saints, along with His own Word and will would come to pass!

As my brother and grandmother arrived at the meeting, Judson Abraham was already praying for people. As they arrived, Judson started praying also for my brother, (in a line? Just along with everyone?) and every time he did, my brother was knocked to the floor. It didn't seem the Holy Spirit was going to allow him to 'just drop my grandmother off!'

After the man of God had prayed a few times for my brother and he continued to fall under the power of the Holy Ghost, Judson Abraham asked him to remove a necklace he was wearing that held an Indian amulet. As soon as my brother removed it, he no longer fell under the power of the Holy Ghost. At that point he decided that he wanted to follow Jesus the Christ.

When he got home, he told my parents about what had happened and they were touched. It was clear to them that this God who had healed our grandmother was now also showing personal interest in other people in our family. That made quite an impression on my parents that God could be that concerned and personal. Here was a God who would heal their grandmother and was willing to pour His Spirit out on one of their children. Who was this God? And why did He have such interest in their family? My parents continued to ponder these unfolding revelations, and my brother began attending church with my grandmother at the Alpha Omega Ministries in Kazipet.

A few months after my older brother had begun attending Christian church, my grandmother told me that she wanted to attend a house meeting, but this time she wanted me to go along with her.

Now I was 11 at that time. I did not want to go to a house meeting with my grandmother and join in a meeting which to me was just a bunch of older people.

But my grandmother was extremely persuasive, telling me there would be food there! A lot of food and good food!! She played every 'bribe card' she held that night, from 'you do not want your grandmother to go alone' to the promise of an abundance of food.

It worked! And soon I found myself walking into a cottage that looked rather unusual on the inside, with about 20 people: the family, their children, the pastor and some older people all singing together.

As we walked in, I realized that maybe the food would come later, as eating didn't seem to be the main purpose of the meeting. I remember being rather bored hearing everyone singing, and so took some time to look around my surroundings. There was not too much to look at that I was familiar with. The inside of their home seemed rather plain compared to the bright colors that adored our family's home with pictures of Hindu gods on the walls, our pujah, or prayer room, as well as our family altar area. No, this place looked decidedly less interesting, I decided, and so just sat next to my grandmother quietly during the singing, not taking too much of an interest in what the adults were doing.

When the singing concluded, the pastor stood up and gave a message from the Bible. This is where the meeting began to take a turn from 'boring' to 'exciting!' After the message a demon-possessed lady who was at the meeting started screaming and shouting. The demon was very angry at the meeting and wanted to do the lady and the meeting great harm. The other adults in the room did not panic, and the pastor rose up in the power of God and commanded the demon to come out in the Mighty Name of Jesus. Very quickly the demon left under command of the Name of Jesus, and the lady lay quietly and peacefully.

WOW!

I had never seen anything like this before! And I have to admit that I was too preoccupied with what I saw to observe it and be thankful for the lady's deliverance. No, I was troubled by what I had seen and became afraid.

"What kind of meeting was this?" "What was the power that the pastor had, and why was that power needed?" I had never seen a demon-possessed person manifesting before and for the 11-year-old who just wanted to eat some good food with his grandmother, it seemed like much, too much to process.

Even though the lady seemed fine, an apprehension came into me. It was unsettling at first, just a low-lying anxiety that I hadn't had before I arrived at the meeting. After the meeting concluded we stayed and ate lunch, as promised, and then made our way back to my parent's home.

When I got home, I went into the washroom to wash my hands to find that although I had walked into the washroom by myself, I was not alone. With no warning, a demon appeared in the washroom and growled 'I am going to kill you!'

I was shocked! What was going on? I quickly responded to him 'why, what have I done?'

The demons gave no reason but continued to repeat that they were going to kill me.

I quickly started asking the gods that our family had prayed to for their protection against these ugly demons. I called on them for a few minutes, but nothing, no one showed up and by this time the demons were laughing at me. It seemed I was in a predicament. I searched my brain for anything I could think of to address these most unusual and most unwelcome visitors.

And then I remembered what I had just seen at the meeting. The pastor had used the Name of Jesus and the demons had to obey that Name!

So, I turned to address the demons directly, saying ''get away from me in the Name of Jesus!''

The instant I said this, I looked and saw absolute horror and shock on the face of these entities. The demons were visibly shaken and now it was their turn to look terrified! I looked at their faces and saw complete horror. Now it was their turn to look traumatized!

It seemed they never expected me to remember the display of power and protection that was in the Name of Jesus that I had seen at the cottage meeting just a short time before. I had just seen His Name defeat the demons who had attacked the woman at the meeting and was just desperate enough to try that Name as well, to see if His Name could protect me as well. .

When I saw the demons' reaction to the Name of Jesus, I was extremely relieved that I found a way out of my dilemma and chanting the Name of Jesus.

I did not know the Bible. I did not know the Lord, but I had heard and seen the power in His Name and it was the only thing I knew to do to keep that terrifying presence of the enemy off me.

After the demon recovered from his shock, he once again turned angry and hateful and said 'ok fine, you have now become smart and know to use the Name of Jesus, and so we will go. But let me tell you this, I am coming back, and I am bringing 7 more with me because your heart is empty.' WOW! I knew nothing of the Bible. I did not know he was quoting Luke 11:26 which says

> [24] "When an impure spirit comes out of a person, it goes through arid places seeking rest and does not find it. Then it says, 'I will return

to the house I left.' 25 When it arrives, it finds the house swept clean and put in order. 26 Then it goes and takes seven other spirits more wicked than itself, and they go in and live there. And the final condition of that person is worse than the first."

As you can imagine, I was still shaking as the demon left and was filled with much fear. I hurriedly ran to my grandmother and told her what happened.

My grandmother was grateful that the Lord had protected me and prayed over me saying 'thank you Lord that you put your own words and Name in the mouth of my grandson, thank you for giving him the ability that is in your Name, thank you for keeping him safe.'

As she prayed, the fear that had come upon me left and my life seemed to go back to how it had been for me. I was grateful that the Name of Jesus had protected me, but I left it at that. I had not heard enough of the gospel proclaimed at this point to understand the reason God sent Jesus to earth. I knew Jesus was powerful, but at the moment did not carry a conviction for my need for a savior.

A few weeks went by, and my parents also attended a church Meeting and they accepted Jesus and became Christian. But I had not done that yet. The Lord was working on every heart in our family, and as His Word says in Philippians 1:6, once He begins something, He will also finish the matter. He will not stop until His work He has planned for our lives is completed.

My entire family started attending a Christian church in our town that met in a two-story building. I am sure that my grandmother and parents were excited that their youngest would be joining them in the faith and thrilled that I was hearing and learning many wonderful Bible stories during the children's church time.

However, this was not happening, not exactly!

The children's church met on the top floor of the building, and once the children were released from the main service, we walked up a flight of stairs to our own service.

But I had other plans! I would sneak out the fire escape before going into the children's service, climb down to the street and play outside, being careful to climb back up the ladder and back into the building and then join the rest of the kids coming down the stairs to meet their parents after the service! As I would walk down the stairs, my mom would beam at me, pleased that her son was learning such wonderful Bible truths!

I felt a tinge of guilt every time I saw her smiling face but had great fear of being caught! It wasn't so much a fear of going to Hell at the time, but it WAS a fear of being caught between my mom and switch! I didn't want to give her any reason to rise up and 'beat the Hell out of me' so to speak, and so every Sunday, avoiding detection of my misdeeds was my top priority.

I was seemingly successful at avoiding the Lord, although the Lord was not content to leave me separated and at arms distance to Him. The Bible says that we did not choose Him, He chose us. Jesus not only sees our great need for Him from a distance, but because He genuinely loves us never stops pursuing us. He will continue orchestrating opportunities for us to hear about His goodness and receive His offer of salvation and eternal Life with Him. And so even though I was skipping out of church every week, the Lord still had the desire, the ability and more importantly a plan to capture my heart for Him.

A few weeks later, still 11 years of age, a man of God came into our town and held a revival not far from our home. The Holy Spirit helped me to understand my position before a Holy God. That I couldn't be in His tangible presence with sin on the inside of me. I did not want to go to Hell, and at this point in my life understood that unless I received Jesus, that is where I would go. It was the first moment of my life that the gospel was clear before me and I understood how I measured up without Christ. I saw my genuine need for Him to forgive and redeem my life and impart to me eternal life so that I could live with God for eternity.

And so finally at this revival, I received the Lord as my savior and had finally had peace about God and my life. I knew that I knew I belonged to Him and that if I died, I would live with Him forever. And at that moment, a large part of my grandmother's prayers had been answered. God had surely saved her entire household, just as He promised. But was there more?

The Bible says that God reveals Himself and teaches us precept upon precept, line upon line. At this point in my life, I knew of the power in the Name of Jesus, I knew my sins had been forgiven and that I belonged to Him. I loved God. But I would not say that I had made a radical decision to make Jesus the pursuit of my life. I was just enjoying my life and being saved. . But that was all about to change.

CHAPTER 2

ENCOUNTERING THE SUPERNATURAL HAND OF THE LORD

I was not a strong student in school. Don't get me wrong, I knew that education was important, especially to my parents, but I was much more interested in having adventures and playing outside. All I wanted to do was play all day, every day, whether school was in session or not.

One day, while still 11, I was just tired of being at school. So, I pretended that I was sick and left school after lunch and came home early. When I got home, my mom was furious to find I had lied to my teachers and left school for no other reason than I didn't want to be there. She was furious! Her and my father had worked hard to provide the best education possible for me and my siblings, and she was not going to allow that to be unappreciated.

She announced that starting immediately I would be not allowed to return to school, and the next day would need to begin to work. Her words cut deep into my heart as she insisted that because of my stunt I did not deserve a good education. I did not deserve to do well in life.

Her words left me physically shaking and fear came and sat in my heart and mind. What was I going to do? As much as I didn't enjoy school, I would much rather be there, then working at the tender age of 11, and was devastated to find myself in this seemingly unavoidable dilemma. And I was fairly sure because of her anger, my mother would make good on those words.

Later that same afternoon, my parents and grandparents went out for some work. I was home by myself and was desperate to escape the inevitable calamity which would befall me in the morning. I was so intimidated that I didn't want to face either my parents or grandma the next morning.

Without a clear plan in mind, but wanting to be anywhere but my home, I grabbed my personal cleaning cup for my bathroom needs, left my house and started to run.

I ran and ran until I got to one of the temples in our town and sat down quietly inside. My mind was racing, and my mind was tormented with fear of punishment from my family. What would become of me?

As I sat in the temple, it was a normal weekday, with people coming and going, but no one taking any special notice or interest in the young boy, who should have been in school, but instead was crouched in fear, wondering in desperation what I should do.

As I sat there, a terrible thought came into my mind that I should end my life. I was a brand-new believer in Jesus, and I didn't know that the enemy had the ability to torment our minds. When the thought came into my mind, I didn't realize it was not my own thought at all, but a fiery dart that the enemy had sent.

As the thought entered my mind, and I didn't know enough to resist it, a strange compulsion led me to leave the temple and go to a train station that was nearby and start climbing up a hill that was right next to the station. It was not a small hill, it was a two mile climb up to the top. As I walked, I didn't feel the peace of God that I had felt a few weeks earlier after receiving Jesus. Instead, I felt driven or under a horrible fear and compulsion to do myself great harm.

When I got to the top, I didn't bother to take time to look around, sit and talk to the Lord, or try to think through what I was going to do next. I looked down the cliff of the hill that I had just climbed and immediately stepped off, expecting immediately to fall quickly and land within seconds on the ground two miles below to my death.

But that didn't happen.

As I jumped, I landed.

But it wasn't on land. I hadn't missed the harrowing cliff and landed on a formerly unseen rock jettying out from the hill. But I landed on what felt like completely solid ground underneath me. And yet when I looked there was nothing there that my eye could see.

I didn't see the angels with my natural eyes, but I knew that they were there the moment I landed on what appeared to be thin air, but, was the hands of the angelic that the Lord had assigned to guard me according to His promise in Psalm 91:11-12

For he shall give his angels charge over thee, to keep thee in all thy ways.

They shall bear thee up in their hands, lest thou dash thy foot against a stone.

I felt myself being slowly lowered all the way back down the cliff I had just climbed, resting in the invisible hands of the angelic hosts. For about 3 seconds I made a gentle ascent downward until I was carefully placed on the ground.

I didn't stop to look around and ask what had happened or who had just helped me. As soon as my feet hit the ground, I continued to run.

I ran almost 16 kilometers, or just under 10 miles until I found myself on a road that was mostly desolated with only a few vehicles passing back and forth. I kept running one foot in front of the other, as a three-wheeler rickshaw drove up next to me. The driver had a hood covering his face, and asked 'do you want a ride?'

'I don't have any money' I confessed, slightly out of breath and slightly bothered that now even this offer of help would be something I would have to turn down.

But my response didn't seem to bother the driver at all. He said that he would be happy to give me a ride, and to hop on. As I did, his face stayed rather obscured, but I couldn't help but notice as I looked at his left mirror, that there was a picture of Jesus. I took my seat, beside him, and as we started to drive, I realized that the tormenting fear was beginning to leave. I started to come back to my senses, although not fully realizing the supernatural events of the last few hours.

We drove for a distance and then he pulled over, on his own account and dropped me off on the side of the road. As I stood there, the vehicle continued down the street and then disappeared in front of my eyes.

At this point, I started to look around and realized to my amazement that I knew where I was. The angelic driver had dropped me off just a few blocks away from my aunt's house. I gathered my composure and walked to her house which was less than 5 minutes away.

When I knocked, she opened the door with the most surprised look on her face I had ever seen. She couldn't grasp how it was that I was standing at her front door. She did not go as far as to close the door in my face, as happened to Peter after his escape from prison, but invited me in quickly realizing that something must be terribly wrong for me to have come that far by myself.

I had never traveled to her home by myself but had always taken a bus with my parents or older siblings. She quickly offered me tea and some homemade bread. My Aunt and cousins were all very concerned to see that I had traveled this distance alone. Gratefully, they were too polite to ask any pointed questions, allowing me to sit and regain my composure from the harrowing experiences of the afternoon.

Unknown to me while I was running through town, one of my parent's neighbors had seen and recognized me. What was I doing so far from my home and why was I running? In concern, they had called my parents. My mom hadn't known where I had run off to, but the Holy Spirit had prompted her to travel to her sister's house. Therefore, no sooner had I begun to calm down at my Aunts, but about 20 minutes later my mother showed up, greatly upset and crying.

My mother was very concerned about me, and the anger she had expressed earlier that day was long gone and only deep compassion for the turmoil I must have gone through. That night my parents took me to our church, and I slept there and slept soundly.

With that experience and the Lord supernaturally sparing my life, my encounter with the angelic to protect me and then escort me in my time of need, the focus of my heart and life instantly and radically shifted.

My heart and attention was now completely focused on Jesus.

I was determined to seek Him with everything that was in me, and to make my life about His purpose for my life. I was finally ready to give God my 100% complete YES. I was finally ready for the Lord to begin to work HIS plan into my life. The plan that my grandmother had prayed over for so many years, asking and believing that God would give her a grandson who would be a man-of-God. Before this day, I had been born-again. But from this day forward, I became obsessed with knowing Jesus and pursuing His powerful Presence and plans for my life.

CHAPTER 3:

MY CALLING IN GOD AND ENCOUNTERING JESUS

Later that year, my father moved our family to Hyderabad, a town that he had been working in for almost 8 years but commuting back and forth. There, my family along with Aunts and Uncles started attending Hermon Gospel Ministries, led by a prophetess who pastored the ministry. The ministry had a salvation system where families would come and spend three days at the church in a type of prayer retreat, drawing near to the Lord and confessing their sins according to 1 John 1:9.

Because this special time of consecration took place over a few days, each family would bring a supply of food for their time of prayer and consecration to the Lord. We would spend the day in prayer and fasting before the Lord and then in the evenings break and prepare simple foods to share in the community, and rest, sleeping at the church, to prepare for the following day of prayer.

It was a very hard system, arising at 4 am for prayer, and meeting in the church with men on one side, women on the other and we would get on our knees and pray until we had a conviction from the Holy Spirit that we were right with the Lord. Our prayers would mirror that of King David's 51st psalm:

> Cleanse me with hyssop, and I will be clean;
> wash me, and I will be whiter than
> snow.
> 8 Let me hear joy and gladness;
>   let the bones you have crushed rejoice.
> 9 Hide your face from my sins
>   and blot out all my iniquity.
> 10 Create in me a pure heart, O God,
>   and renew a steadfast spirit within me.
> 11 Do not cast me from your presence
>   or take your Holy Spirit from me.
> 12 Restore to me the joy of your salvation
>   and grant me a willing spirit, to sustain me.

This time was a time of consecration and sanctification before the Lord, and it fit our family well. Our family had been devout Hindu's not missing a day of prayer, and my parents wanted to assure that we were now just as devoted and committed to the One True God.

During these days I started to struggle with finding things to confess. I was still a young boy and had gladly given my life to Jesus after He had spared my life so miraculously and was crazy in love with Him. Because I did not know the Word in great detail and hadn't lived too terribly long to do much great sin, after a few hours of prayer I couldn't find much else to confess. But my heart was very hungry for the Lord. I wanted to know Him Personally. I wanted to interact with Him, and see His power displayed in my life. So that became my personal focus once I felt my heart was right with the Lord during this time of prayer.

We stayed at the church all Thursday and prayed.

We then spent all Friday praying as well.

On Saturday afternoon about 4pm everyone had finished praying for the day and left the prayer room to join in the community kitchen and prepare the evening food. I realized it would be a very peaceful time to be in the church by myself, and so I snuck away from the group and entered the sanctuary quietly. I loved the Presence of God and wanted to spend some intimate time with Him seeking Him and hearing His heart and voice for my life.

I knelt on the floor, in the quiet of the room and began to pray, speaking to the Lord, praising Him, and worshiping His Son Jesus.

As I began to pray, I suddenly heard a voice calling out 'Samuel, Samuel.'

I opened my eyes, expecting to see a person that might have entered the room after I had. But there was no one there.

So, I closed my eyes and returned to prayer. No sooner had I done so, when again I heard the same voice call out 'Samuel, Samuel.'

I opened my eyes in the small sanctuary, again convinced that someone had quietly walked in, and although perhaps obscured from my sight, was standing, calling out. But as my eyes scanned the four walls of the room, I realized that I was still alone praying.

This third time, as I returned to prayer, the voice came one more time, only this time I also heard great thunder, and from the thunder an authoritative voice calling out 'Samuel, Samuel'.

This time, I did not take time to look around the room for a human visitor, but instead addressed the Lord directly.

'Lord, I know you are trying to speak to me' I responded. 'But my name is not Samuel, it is Nagasai Vardhan.'

With my realization that I was now in conversation with the Lord, God wasted no time in communicating His reason for His visitation.

'I am calling you as a prophet to the nations and you will be my witness all around the world. I am going to use you and I have chosen you before the foundation of the world. I will use you and I will take you around the world.'

As the Lord released His call on my life, I remained kneeled in awe and silence with my heart pounding and everything in my spirit alive to the Living God. The Lord had moved and spoken according to His own Word in Jeremiah 1:5 and in answer to my grandmother's prayers that He send her a grandchild who would be a man of God, used mightily in the plan of God for the last days before His return.

My face started to glow and shine with yellow glory light. I remained in the sanctuary for a time, and then returned to the rest of the group preparing the evening meal. When the prophetess inquired about my countenance, I briefly told her of the encounter.

The rest of the afternoon seemed to pass quickly as did the evening and the next day being Sunday, I found myself back in the church building, only this time with the Prophetess and rest of the families holding our weekly meeting. The service started at noon and usually lasted until about 3 or 4 that afternoon.

As the service started, I was still contemplating the Lord's call on my life. I was very joyful, and word had begun to spread in the church that God had spoken to me. Some people were very excited about it, while others wondered 'why him?' About half-way into the service, during the preaching, about 2:15pm, I was sitting with my eyes open, when I suddenly saw two angels coming down from heaven, with no wings. They stood before me bringing with them a living beam of light, golden, bright light carried me up into the heavens into a realm and location of glory and the heavenly Presence of God. As we traveled upward, I was aware we were heading to a wonderful destination, and I was both excited and peaceful to be in the Presence of these heavenly hosts.

When we arrived, I found myself standing in a heavenly place with the most beautiful Person I had ever seen standing before me. He was handsome and beautiful with a radiance of love and compassion and strength and understanding. As I caught sight of Him, my heart leapt as my eyes beheld Him. His appearance and countenance defied any words that I know or have ever learned. He emulated the highest level of all these words and yet encapsulates galaxies past what our understanding of any of these words are.

As I gazed upon Him, He was glorious, beautiful, majestic, fetching, handsome, holy, radiant, glowing, compelling, magnetic, eternal, kingly, royal, sovereign, excellent, above all things, kind, loving, eternally patient and kind. He was so completely God and so completely man at the same time, it was difficult to take in everything I was seeing. I felt instantly pulled to Him and wanted to get as close as possible.

I asked, ``Are you Jesus?"

He answered 'Yes I am.'

I replied "I admire you Jesus, I love and am in amazement of you, can I touch you?'

He replied, 'Yes, you can.'

I reached out and touched His garment and electricity went through my body from His magnificent Presence.

He was so filled with glory, and it was so glorious to behold Him, that it seems difficult to believe that I could notice anything else but Him. But as I stood there gazing at His face, I could see from His right side a flash of lightning and a person walking with a crown on their head that was filled with the most beautiful diamonds I had ever seen.

When I saw this other person, crowned with opulent diamonds, I asked the Lord what the crown was for. He said that whoever saves souls on the earth, would have diamonds on their crown in heaven.

He then continued to speak to me, telling me "I have chosen you for a great purpose. I have chosen you for a big purpose.'

Then the Lord looked at me and said 'I want to give you something'

I put my hands out, expecting Him to put something in them. But instead of doing so, He opened His mouth and breathed into me. I could feel His breath and very substance go deep into my body, penetrating my spirit man on the inside.

"All I have done; you are going to do." He said "As I have laid my hands on others you are going to do the same. You will do the same things that I have done, and you will do greater.' I was standing there rather not knowing how to respond, just soaking up every word and breath that He breathed when he then called Peter over.

I turned and saw Peter, one of the first apostles of the New Testament church walk over to where we were standing. 'Give me the key' He instructed him. I could see that Peter was holding what appeared to be a gold key, shining and shimmering as if polished gold.

"This is the key to the church' Jesus announced. "I gave it to Peter and now I am giving it to you.'

As He handed me the key He continued to speak and instruct me.

"Be humble," He said. 'This is of great importance."

"I am going to use you and through you I will come a second time and will continue to use you in Jerusalem and all around the world.'

When the Lord finished giving me instructions, the two angelic hosts who had carried me into the heavens, then took me and transported me through a beam of light back into the meeting that was almost over. No one at the meeting had been aware of the encounter that I had experienced. My body had remained seated in the pew listening to the message while the Lord had called me up into the heavens. I sat there in utter amazement and gratitude to the Lord.

It would be impossible for my life to ever be the same again.

CHAPTER 4:
TIMES OF TRIAL

O ne of the results of this encounter was that from the moment of my return, I found that my spiritual eyes were completely open. I started to see everything around me clearly, both what the Lord was doing, but also, I could see sickness and disease around me, and I was not sure what to do about what I was seeing. Therefore, although the encounter with the Lord was glorious, the season that followed was challenging.

I did not have a grid for seeing into the spirit. I talked to the church about this encounter and asked the Prophetess/Pastor for her counsel on how to navigate this newfound spiritual eyesight. The prophetess had not had similar encounters nor had the Lord opened her eyes in the same manner, so she was unclear how to advise and counsel me. It was also a challenge for envy and jealousy to not set in with some of the people in our church, and so I found myself a bit between a hard place and a rock. I was grateful for the encounter, but now carried fear whenever I went because of what I was seeing in the spirit. That, added to having little or no support on how to handle this reality, left me struggling in those 2 years that followed.

At the age of 14, a prophetess from Australia came to Hyderabad for some services. I attended one of them and went up front to have her pray over me. As I stood in front of her the Lord began to show her my life and the purpose that He had called me to.

"You are a prophet," she said, 'and the streets of Jerusalem are waiting for you.' She then told me the encounter that I had had in heaven with the Lord and how He had given me the gold key that He had given Peter and His instructions to me.

'The reason for this call," she continued, "and the reason you are who you are before God is that your grandmother had asked the Lord for Him to send her a man of God into her family.' She also then went on to describe the scene of my birth, that the Lord showed her, that as I was born, the nurse that attended my birth dedicated me into the ministry as an infant.

'But in the years to follow' she continued, 'when you are 15, 16, 17, 18 and 19 you will face many oppositions.

'At one point everyone will be against you. They will speak poorly about your character, and you will be broken completely. You will try to end your own life 7 times.'

The words were delivered with the anointing of the Holy Spirit, as part of His ministry written in John 16:13, that He is called the Spirit of Truth, He will guide us into all truth, and will show or reveal to us the things to come.' And some of the things to come, the Lord will show us, for us to pray those attacks of the adversary away. But other instances as when the Lord dealt with Paul in showing him things that he would have to suffer for His name's sake, some things the Lord shows us we will not be able to pray away.

However, the Lord is good to tell us ahead of time things that we will suffer, so that when they unfold, we are prepared and know that just like He saw the difficulty up ahead, He also has already planned and prepared a way through. 2 Cor. 12: 7-9

To keep me from becoming conceited because of these surpassingly great revelations, there was given me a thorn in my flesh, a messenger of Satan, to torment me. Three times I pleaded with the Lord to take it away from me. But he said to me, "My grace is sufficient for you, for my power is made perfect in weakness." Therefore, I will boast all the more gladly about my weaknesses, so that Christ's power may rest on me.

And so, I can't say that these prophetic words were comforting words, but they were accurate words. For about a years' time from then I would find myself entering the lowest period of my life. But before this drama had begun to unfold and these prophetic words came to pass, there was another issue I faced and revelation that God wanted to impart to me, to ensure my heart was prepared for the trials that were up ahead.

During this same season, after the encounter in heaven, my older brother got effected by witchcraft and became very sick. This drew me even closer to God. Even after the encounter in heaven, and I had seen the Lord, I still had a lingering thought in my heart that God was an angry God. I knew that Jesus was brilliant and kind, but there was a lingering thought below the surface of my heart that perhaps God was angry and was much harder to get along with.

But as I saw my brother suffering firsthand, I found I carried a deep compassion for him. God started ministering directly to me in that season, helping me to see that just as I had a deep compassion for my brother, God had that same deep compassion and concern about me. God was not just supernatural and filled with power.

45

God was love.

God had a Father's heart.

God looked upon me with the same compassion as a concerned Father would have for His son. I had known the kind heart of a Father, from my earthly father, and now my heart became convinced that God's heart was supernaturally kind as a Father's as well. That was a powerful revelation, and one I would need for the next season ahead.

In the years right after the powerful encounter I had with Jesus in heaven, I spent a large part of each day on the streets of India, preaching the gospel, casting out demons and seeing the sick healed. As the prophetic word had stated that I would enter a season where everyone would turn against me, at the age of 19 this situation began to unfold.

I was working in a ministry as an usher, and at that time, a false accusation was brought against me while working in a ministry as usher. Because the adversary was using this lie to try to undo the ministry that the Lord had called me to, the lie spread swiftly through many churches in our area. Instead of stopping the rumor, when one person heard it, people passed the rumor along. Instead of asking the Lord to tell them if the lie was true or false, people believed the lie. There was not much I could do to defend myself against people's hearts when they turned against me. It was just as the prophetic word had stated that everyone would turn away from me. I found myself living in a season when I walked down the street, people would spit on the ground when they saw me coming.

Before this accusation was made, I had already started to receive many invitations to speak at churches. But after the false rumor was spread, I tried to visit 15 of these churches where I had been invited, and each time was physically grabbed and removed and told that I could not be there.

My heart was broken on the inside.

I had a very difficult time reconciling my great love for the Lord and the desire to have Him move and touch people through my life, and the cold and judgmental response I was currently getting from people in the religious community. I knew the Lord and loved the Lord and knew He loved me deeply. But at the same time, I was experiencing great judgment from the people who said they knew Him.

I saw great amounts of cold heartedness rather than the love of God demonstrated to me in that season. Four times I had a pastors spit in my face. These were the same pastors who stood in their pulpits on Sundays and spoke of the love of God. Those days continued to drive me closer into the deep places in the heart of God. His angels continued to minister to me, just like they ministered to Him when He faced rejection and accusation from His own people.

Ever since the encounter He had given me in heaven, I had spent my days walking the streets of Hyderabad preaching on the street corners and praying for the sick. And I found much comfort and solace in that. I found my heart slowly regaining strength as I allowed my heart to continue to pursue and be consumed by the Lord and love of spreading His powerful gospel. And remember that His Word says that when any of us go and proclaim His Word and good news of the gospel, that He goes with us, and confirms the Word that we speak about Him with signs and wonders following. I knew He was with me on the streets and could feel His heart for the broken and lost as I sat among them praying and ministering out His power to heal.

So I learned to love this way of life of getting out of the walls of the church, which were for the moment, a place I was not welcomed, nor wanted, and spent my days with the Lord, sowing them on the streets of India. For the five years since my encounter in heaven, I spent many happy hours with the Lord spreading the gospel and see-ing Him heal the sick.

As I exercised my faith day after day, I saw the Lord heal every matter of disease from leprosy to AIDS, to blindness and deafness. The streets of India were filled with men and women suffering from serious illness where there was no medical treatment available. And so it be-came routine in the grandest of ways to see the Lord walk with us and heal scores and scores of the blind, deaf, lame and poor. There was nothing that we did not see the Lord heal and heal in great quantities.

The streets had become a sanctuary of sorts and my place of walking, talking and partnering with the Lord. He had told me in the encounter in heaven that I would do what He had done, and Acts 10:38 says that He walked around a town, doing good and healing all who were op-pressed of the devil, for God was with Him. He had given me a sincere love for the hurt and hidden, and the burden to relieve the suffering of others by sharing the love and power of Jesus to save and to heal completely.

Therefore, in the days of ostracization by the pastors and churches in my area, I had found rest for my soul on the streets of India, ministering the love of Jesus to those who also were separated from the churches, but whose hearts were hungry for the Lord and gladly received the good news of salvation. I spent many afternoons sitting on the sidewalks, talking to those also sitting on the streets about their concerns and showing them that Jesus cared about their need to be healed and would heal them. My heart began to heal and grow stronger day by day.

I didn't really expect the Lord to give me any more encounters with Him, He had already done so much for me in such a few years. But the Bible says that the heart of God is always to do more than we can ask, think, or imagine. And sometimes it is not the more than we can ask miracles that the Lord wants to deposit. Sometimes 'the more' that He wants to do is more personal. Sometimes it is not about performing one more miracle.

Sometimes God's supernatural is about greater intimacy with Him.

CHAPTER 5:

LUNCH WITH GOD

One day, in this season in which my heart was still mending from the ostracization from the churches in our area, the Lord came to me and said, 'Do you want to have lunch with me today?'

I said 'yes.'

He told me then to ride my Motorcycle to a certain location and stop at a hotel to buy biryani (rice with chicken). He then directed me to a second place to buy water and Paper Plate then gave me a third location for our lunch appointment. As I got to a certain place, He said 'stop here.'

I got off my bike and looked around and saw no one on the street except a beggar standing in tattered rags not too far away on the side of the street. It was evident that he had been staying at the location on the street for some time. There was excrement all around him, as he had used the area around him to relieve himself. I could see the dried up remains all around him. He was standing quite unaware of me, with saliva coming out of his mouth. The odor coming from him and the ground around him was strong and foul, and it was the last place that I wanted to eat lunch.

But the Lord instructed me to walk over to the man, get the rice and food that I had bought out of my sack and put on a plate. I did so and then took my hand and cleared the saliva from his mouth and with my hand scooped up some of the rice and chicken and brought it to his mouth, one time, two times, three times.

After the third time, the Lord said, 'You eat now.' But I didn't want to. As I started to also eat from the same plate, and the man continued to eat as well, saliva from the man's mouth started to fall on the plate and mix into some of the food.

The Lord told me to take my hand and separate on the plate the food with the saliva away from the food that had no saliva in it. Then God said 'take the good food that has no saliva in it and give that food to the man. You eat the food that has saliva in it.'

I was feeling very poorly by this time. Emotionally, I was feeling very low and like I was not really enjoying this lunch that the Lord had invited me to. But as I was aware of these emotions, I also was aware that I had nothing bad to say against God. There was nothing bad that God had ever done or said to me, and I did not want to say anything bad about what He was telling me to do.

It was a difficult lunch for me to eat.

Besides the saliva being mixed in the food, the odor from human excrement was so strong that it was hard not to taste the odor as I ate the remaining food on the plate. After we finished eating and sharing our meal together, I took some of the water that I had brought with me and washed my hands as well as the face of my beggar friend, carefully removing the saliva.

As I finished, I remember I had another unopened bottle of water that I wanted to leave with him. I turned to my satchel and grabbed it off the top, but when I turned around just a second later, the man had completely disappeared!

At the same exact moment that I saw he was not there, I heard the voice of the Lord:

'You just ate lunch with Me.'

In my heart was a glorious presence, a fiery love burning very strong as He spoke those words to me. I could feel His deep and powerful love for me, and my love for Him.

In Matthew 25 Jesus was talking to a group of followers encouraging them that there will be a reward seat they will stand in front of God's throne one day. He will tell them thank you for all of the times that He was hungry, and they fed Him and thirsty and He gave them something to drink. When they ask, 'but Lord, when did we ever see you hungry or thirsty and feed you?' He said that anytime they had fed or given food to the hungry, they had done that unto Him. God can do anything that He says He can in His Word. It is very true that the Lord will allow us to interact with Him on earth, by following His Word and instruction and tending to the needs of the poor. What we do unto them, we do unto Him. And there are times in which He will allow us to see and interact with Him directly.

As my heart was filled with the glory and love of God, Jesus continued to speak to me.

'I am giving you this cloud, My cloud. It is the cloud of my Presence. It is the same cloud that I gave to the Israelites. Wherever you are, you can see this cloud, whether it is daytime or nighttime.'

God gave me this wonderful gift out of His heart for me as a reward for my obedience and desire to do what He asked of me, no matter how difficult or how much part of me did not want to do what He asked.

God will do the same for you.

Anytime, He asks us to serve in a difficult place or in a manner that is difficult for us, He always rewards us with the glory of His Presence. God is rewarder of those who diligently seek Him.

With this astonishing encounter, and my heart filled with the fire, love and Presence of God, I continued to completely immerse myself into my calling and position before the Lord. And it was not soon after that encounter that the painful days I had walked out of seemed far behind me. In the months and years that followed, the Lord was very gracious to me and indeed confirmed His Word to me that the cloud of His Presence was always with me, and as I preached His Word, He would confirm that Word with signs and wonders following.

During those years, the Lord was faithful to open door after door both for street evangelism but also for church meetings and crusades. We saw the Lord reach over 120,000 people in those years, many of them drug dealers that once they encountered the power of God, they were set free in their hearts and from addictions.

1 Corinthians 3:6 says that one sows, one waters, but it is the Lord who causes the growth. So, in those days, my focus was evangelism and getting the gospel spread. Doing the work of the evangelist, which is to throw out a wide net and catch as many fish in the area as possible. The Lord told me to stay busy in that part of my calling and let Him use those around us to do the discipling and pastoring at that time. That sat very well with me! I wanted to be 'out of the church building' actively partnering with the Lord and seeing Him do what He did when He walked the earth.

Honestly, one of my greatest concerns was that I wanted to avoid sitting inside of a church so long that I would start to look like part of the building, like part of a museum, just sitting there looking polished and pretty, but not accomplishing anything for the Lord. I didn't want to get caught in the trap that I saw some Christians had that I had met early in my ministry years. There were groups of believers in my early ministry days that when they saw the fire and passion of God in my life, would sit back in their chairs, and say wistfully, 'oh yes, I remember fondly the days of my youth when I "had" such passion for the Lord.'

I never wanted my passion and fire to be in the rear-view mirror!

I didn't want to ever have to say 'the passion I 'once had.' No, I wanted the fire and purpose of God to be the very heartbeat of my life for today and every day after that until He returned! I wanted to pursue His kingdom above all, and His love be my consuming passion. I never wanted to stop pressing into greater depths of His glory and manifestations of His power! For Jesus and His Kingdom truly ARE worthy of our pursuit with all of our heart, soul, mind, and strength, amen!

In those early ministry years, the Lord taught me how to operate in and depend on words of knowledge and His voice to know where to go and what to do when I got there. Just as His Son Jesus spent evenings praying and receiving instructions about what town to travel to the next day, and what message to bring the people when He got there, we would pray as well and the Lord would tell us to get on this bus or that. When we arrived at our destination, He would tell us how to engage the people there, many times using a prophetic word to open a person's heart to believe that God was real, that He knew them, cared about them and had something specific He wanted to tell them.

As we traveled and talked to people, whether old or young, the Lord would tell us such hidden secrets from the name of a loved one, to something they were asking the Lord about, to the inside of their homes, or a plan that the Lord had for them. He always gave us very specific words, many times showing us a flash in the spirit of what He was seeing and then having us describe it to them.

At meetings He would give us words about estranged family members, birthdays, financial situations, hidden health problems. He wanted us to represent Him, as Jesus represented Him. Remember, the Bible says that the gospel is a gospel of power and demonstration. And Jesus commanded His disciples to wait in Jerusalem for the empowerment of the Holy Spirit before taking the message of salvation to the world. He didn't want people just walking around saying 'there is a God.' He wanted you and I equipped with the same empowerment that He walked in, to demonstrate that God saw each person on earth, knew how many hairs were on their head and every hidden detail of their past, present and future.

So just as Jesus walked down the street and the Holy Spirit would point out a man and tell Jesus that His name was 'Zacchaeus' and to go to his house that day, so we would walk down streets or be in meetings and the Holy Spirit point out hundreds of hundreds of people and give me details about their names, situations and other concrete details so that people would know God is real and that He was Immanuel, God with them. God wants the lost to know He is good and knows everything about their lives. And He wants His church empowered and equipped to go out and be Jesus to their neighborhoods and the nations.

As meeting after meeting unfolded, I grew in my ability to operate in greater and greater amounts of the grace for my calling, the Lord continued to remind me that He had promised He would use me for BIG things. He would use me in BIG places. He would operate through the nations through me. Many nations, not just one or two, here or there. My heart continued to grow in Him and the things of the spirit and continued to enlarge and believe this Word He had spoken over me.

When the Lord spoke to me about the nations, it ignited an increased desire in myself to see anything that was around me in my home country healed by the power of God. I pursued seeing leprosy, AIDS, stroke, paralysis, accidents and many creative miracles, new kidneys, new hearts completely healed where there had been stunts in hearts, we saw the Lord replace the stint with original parts. God was moving through us in mighty ways in the mighty Name of Jesus!

It was not often, but sometimes I would meet a person who had a disease that was so advanced and crippling that it would even shock me. But the Lord taught me that when that happened, I was to say 'But God, I trust YOU, and I believe in YOU' and then start to speak directly TO the condition it in the mighty name of Jesus. I thoroughly enjoyed every day of ministry partnered with the Lord. I have thousands of scenes of His goodness imprinted in my heart for eternity. I have been blessed to see thousands of people healed by the power of Jesus. And I been blessed to see the Holy Spirit minister prophetic words of knowledge, words of wisdom, and all manner of encouraging words.

The Lord had been so gracious to me to this point of my life! He had been so faithful to allow me to see what He promised me I would be allowed to see Him do.

Jesus had already walked with me and allowed me to walk in so much of the ministry that He walked in.

But in a few years, my heart started to focus on His specific words that I would do EVERYTHING that He did.

And so, I started to inquire of Him about raising the dead.

CHAPTER 6:

CHAPTER 6:

RAISING THE DEAD

I have told my friends around the world many times that India is different from many nations. In India you can't just walk up to someone and say, 'God wants to bless you.' Because they will take you to task and say 'ok, good, if He told you this, then HOW is He going to bless me and WHEN is He going to bless me?' People in India want to HEAR God say something specific, and want to see Him DO something specific, not just put a general blessing on their life.

Christian tradition is that St. Thomas traveled to India, arriving in 52 A.D. and was the first disciple to preach the gospel in India, heal people of many sicknesses and diseases and bring people to a saving faith in Jesus. We do not have a firsthand account of this in the Bible, but we do have an ample supply of historical writings that chronicle his arrival and ministry in the subcontinent of India.

And remember who Thomas was and the record we have in the Bible. He was called 'doubting Thomas.' He was the disciple that said, 'unless I see the scars on Jesus' hands I will not believe.' In other words, 'show me something, do not just tell me, and I will believe.'

Because Thomas' heart or thought pattern required outward evidence of what God had done through Jesus, it is likely that his ministry was marked with well documented and easy to recognize miracles. If Thomas required this for himself, then he most likely pulled on the anointing and learned to operate in great faith so that he could demonstrate real healing miracles that even a doubt prone people could not deny.

Hence, we have the very foundation of HOW India was evangelized! With GREAT signs and wonders of blind eyes opening, deaf ears hearing, the lame walking, the dead raised, and the gospel preached to the poor. It was as if India was first exposed to great signs and wonders that accompanied the preaching of the Word, and that desire to see them, or the standard or necessity to have them has never left that people group.

That was certainly the case for me personally. I did not want to just read about the power of God to raise the dead, I wanted to see God raise the dead!

The Bible said He could do it! The Bible said that I could do the same things that He had done and greater. And Jesus Personally had spoken to me in the heavenly encounter and said that I would do the exact things that He had done. So I was in full faith to see Jesus raise the dead!

To build my faith, I had spent a season meditating on the account in the Bible about Jesus raising the dead. I poured over the account of Jesus raising Lazarus and the widow's son. I searched out the account of Paul raising the young man who had fallen from the window as well as the accounts of Elijah and Elisha raising the dead under the Old Covenant. The more I meditated on God's ability to raise a dead person, the stronger my faith became.

One day, filled with the faith that comes from feeding on the Word, I went to a friend of mine and announced, 'I am fully expecting God to raise the dead through me, He is going to help me do it.'

That person believed me.

It was not too much longer after we spoke that he arranged for me to connect to a family he knew that had just had a family member pass. It was a 68-year-old woman who had been sick for a while and who had been expected to die. To me and my friend in faith, a dead person was a dead person, and there seemed no reason not to expect God to instantly raise that person up!

As I arrived at the home, I could see that the body of this older woman had been laid out in front of the home, as is custom in India. She had passed earlier that morning, and it was already the afternoon when I arrived. Her body had not yet discolored, nor started bloating and she lay rather peacefully on the ground. In my mind's eyes I could easily see me laying hands on this precious grand-mother and then she instantly sitting up and returning to her family who loved her.

I walked over and kneeled and gently laid my hand on her. I knew Jesus loved her and knew that Jesus would help me. He had always helped me every time I prayed for a sick person, this situation I figured would be no differ-ent.

As I laid my hand, I started to thank the Lord for rais-ing her and then started to command her to return in the mighty name of Jesus. I knew His name well! I had seen the power and might of that Name heal instantly over and over. I expected His Name to instantly touch and heal blindness, deafness, leprosy, lameness of all kinds, AIDS, and it always did.

But this time as I lay my hands on this sweet older grandmother and commanded her back in the name of Jesus, nothing happened!

I was shocked!

I had never seen nothing happen!

What was going on???

I felt irritated that my faith and the power of God had not instantly brought life and breath into her lungs. I raised my voice and decided instead of giving into frustration, I would press in with even greater determination and zeal!

'I COMMAND YOU!' I yelled, 'to come BACK in the mighty Name of JESUS!' The zeal inside of me welled up, and I kept this loud command up over and over. If she was not going to respond, I was determined to make her respond!

But nothing happened.

As time passed, and I continued to loudly give commands for her to raise, I could feel my strength slowly giving way to fatigue. At this point, because of the decibel level, and probably the rather unusual sight of someone praying for a dead person, there was quite a crowd around watching. They were the grandmother's family members, but also friends of the family that had come to pay their respects.

They were all standing around, not exactly sure how to respond. Most of them were from a different faith tradition and so were not joining in with me 'agreeing with my faith' or praying in unison under their breaths. As the minutes ticked by, I became less aware of the Holy Spirit moving in me and increasingly aware of the crowd standing around me. Although I was exercising every bit of faith from the Word and Name of Jesus I could pull on, I suspected that in the eyes of many I might begin to appear like the crazy person in this situation.

The family was exceedingly gracious and allowed me to continue to pray for three or four hours. I was grateful. I knew the faith I carried was genuine faith, I knew the Lord would do what He said. But after a few hours I had reached a state of shock that she had not raised. It seemed more plausible to me that she was raised, than remained dead, and I really couldn't reconcile or understand why I was not seeing it.

The family came over and told me that they knew that God could and would raise the dead, but they felt that He would raise a different person, on a different day and requested that I stop praying so that they could bury her body.

I was a bit green in 'raising the dead' protocol. I had not planned for any type of scenario where the person did NOT come back, and so hadn't thought out ahead of time a well phrased response.

Out of my fatigue and inevitable disappointment, I responded "you do not have faith for God to raise her?' It came out more of an accusation than anything, which I did not intend, but I was determined to hold onto my faith, and so was trying to separate their response from what I wanted to do, which was to keep praying.

They were very upset when I said this. It had been a long and trying day for them as well, and everyone's nerves were on their last straw.

'You gave us false hope' they yelled back. 'You told us that if you prayed, the person would come back to life!'

And out of their grief and disappointment they began to beat me. And because there were many of them, and they believed I had given them false hope, they beat me very badly. I crouched down with my hands over me trying to cover my face, and they continued to beat on me until blood started to flow down my face. They were an angry mob at this point, with many of them kicking me and hurling insults at me for being a false person.

Finally, after a time, the mob drew back, and they addressed me.

'If you pray for anyone else, if we find out that you go and tell anyone else that you will pray for them to be raised and they are not raised, we will find you and we will kill you.'

I was relieved that the beating had stopped and sincerely and humbly addressed them all and apologized for giving them false hope. I was truly sorry for the pain they were experiencing. I knew Jesus and I knew He was trustworthy, so I was able to remain calm as the hours had ticked by while I prayed, but they did not know Jesus personally. Because they did not carry the hope that the Lord Jesus imparts into the hearts of believers and so their hopes had been dashed and their emotions had run high.

I couldn't blame them for being upset. There are many situations in life which are very difficult to handle and endure without faith in Jesus, and the death of a loved one is certainly one of them. And it is the exact reason why I used every ounce of faith I had and why I so desperately wanted this family to see the power of God. I wanted them to know the Lord for who He was and what He could do.

I thanked them again for allowing me to pray for their grandmother and left their home with blood running down my face and on my body. I felt weak. I walked to a hotel and ordered a chai tea.

I sank into my chair, exhausted and bloodied, with my tea. As I began to drink, drops of blood from my face fell into my cup of tea. As they did, the Lord opened my spiritual eyes to a vision, and I was allowed to see the throne of God and the blood flowing down Jesus' face when the crown of thorns was adhered to His head. I could see both the power of God and His complete victory over all, as well as the price that it cost Him Personally.

My heart sank deeply and gratefully into what God was showing me. It was a place of complete resting and comfort in the Lord.

And in response to what He showed me, the Holy Spirit comforted me. And gave me the revelation which arose quietly in my spirit, 'I can fail, but Jesus never fails.'

Chapter 7:

Pressing into Raising the Dead

I recovered from the beating, allowed myself time to build my faith up strongly again and then soon found another dead person to pray for. I followed the same basic routine I had the first time, praying and commanding them to rise in the mighty name of Jesus. And again, I failed three more times.

In each of these situations, I prayed until the family asked me to stop. And then when the person had not been raised, I received a sure and swift beating from the family.

It really had not occurred to me yet that there might be more dynamics in play in raising the dead than just my own faith. In each of these situations, I was praying for families who did not share the same Christian faith that I did, but I was assuming that the Lord would raise the dead on my faith alone. That did not seem to be the case, at least not for these first four people I prayed for.

But the fourth person that I prayed for was different. In 2015 I went to visit a Christian family who carried strong faith in Jesus. While I was visiting their home, we got word that their neighbor, an elderly gentleman, had passed. The family I was visiting said 'why don't you go pray for him?' They believed that the Lord could raise him.

The problem was that I did not have faith at that moment. I had failed four times before. I didn't really want to go next door and pray for this man as well.

But the couple I was visiting was very kind and had asked me to go and see if I could help. And so, I collected myself and gathered all of the courage I could muster and walked next door.

When I got to the next door and saw the gentleman, he appeared to be 78 or 80. My first thought was 'what will be the use of raising him, he is so old anyway he will not live long even if we bring him back.'

As I stepped close to this man, lying on the ground, God said 'go and slap his dead body.'

I was rather taken back by hearing this. I approached his body casually and leaned over it and put my hand on his face and started to gently rub his face instead of slapping him.

I was thinking to myself that there was a possibility that the adversary had told me to slap him, just so he could watch me fail a fifth time and receive another unwanted beating. Although I was willing to pray and believe Jesus' part of my heart in that moment was still carrying a thought that I would fail again and I wasn't sure how much more humiliation I could take.

But then the Lord repeated His instructions. 'Slap his dead body.'

This time I replied, 'ok Lord, if you say to do this, I will do this.'

Before I did, I turned his neck in my hand this way and that, allowing me to look across both sides of the room, and quickly counted the number of people that had gathered to watch. I counted about 15 people in the room and calculated that if each person slapped me 2 times, that would be about 30 hits against me. You can tell that in my heart, I was willing to obey the Lord, but I still was expecting that I would fail again as I had before.

I took a deep breath, pulled on every ounce of faith I had and slapped the person with as much energy as I could and then before anyone else could move a muscle,

I threw myself in the corner of the room and crouched down with my hands over my head, anticipating the blows to begin.

But instead, I heard a deep gasp of air and a loud breath being drawn!

I opened my eyes and saw that he had come back to life and was breathing! I was in shock! Everyone in the room was in shock! He sat up and started talking to his family. I stood there rather stunned and not sure what to say or do.

His family members started walking over to me one by one, shaking my hand and thanking me. I was in such a state of shock, it was all I could do to keep my composure, shake hands and say, 'praise the Lord!' I went home that afternoon praising God with everything in me. I was so grateful to the Lord for doing this miracle and filled with God's joy of seeing the man reunited with his family. It had been an over and above afternoon, much more than I could have asked for, thought about or expected!

That night I kept thanking and praising the Lord! My love for Him and consecration to Him to believe Him to raise the dead grew to a higher level than ever before. I was experiencing the deepest joy and gratitude and intimacy with the Lord and fellowship with Him that I had to that point of my life. He had shown Himself to be faithful to answer my heart's request to see Him raise the dead. I was deeply thankful and deeply in awe of His power.

There were a few consequences to Jesus raising that man. The first was that a few people started talking about it as word traveled about what the Lord had done. The second was that almost overnight pride entered my heart and I started to think 'wow, I can raise the dead!' Those two consequences did not mix very well. On one hand, other people wanted to see me raise the dead and so started inviting me to pray for this person and that. At the same time, I was thinking 'ok this is my ministry now, everyone I pray for will come back, this is going to be impressive! I now know what I am doing!'

I still carried faith, but also carried pride and the next few instances were disastrous. In fact, in the next few months while praying for a sick person, I lay my hand on their head and just as I did, they STOPPED breathing and DIED! I kept praying for people and three other people died just in similar manner, with me laying my hands on their head and then they stopped breathing.

It seems like an ironic and almost humorous account years later that I had had such an incredible experience with the Lord and then faced such failure. But those were important years where the Lord was teaching me, training me, correcting me, and helping me to understand what condition He needed my heart to be in so that He could move through me.

When we belong to the Lord and are in a season of training and seeking and pursuing Him for gifts of healing or miracles, it is not wasted time. It sometimes requires us to stay in faith over a season longer than we had planned, for the Lord to mold and prepare our heart for what we are believing Him to see.

And this was certainly the case in my life. If there is anything I could write to encourage you, my believing friend who also has a hunger to see the supernatural power of God demonstrated in tangible ways, it is to not quit. Hebrews 10:35 says that we are not to throw away the confidence that we had at first, for it will bring us a great reward if we persevere in our faith. And anything of God that we have a deep desire to pursue and walk in the Lord will teach us how to do so, if we faint not.

If we stand through the persecution and obstacles and battles of faith on our end, the Lord's desire for us will prevail. Each of us is unique and we will each have unique hearts that the Lord has to deal with and instruct us, as each of us pursue the miracle realm of God. Do not allow yourself to stay discouraged when setbacks come, because they will. But learning how to have faith in God, not in our own ability, will yield great dividends.

During this season, the most important realization I came to was that even though I carried faith to raise the dead, I realized finally 'I cannot raise the dead. Jesus alone can raise the dead.' This was not just a mental belief or philosophical position. I knew that I knew this in my heart from years of praying for people to be raised. I knew God could do it and knew I could not.

And once I got to that place in my heart, it was amazing what unfolded after that.

CHAPTER 8:

THE SUPERNATURAL POWER OF GOD

The most important revelation I carried at this time was that all the glory for raising the dead belongs to Jesus. There is nothing that we can do as humankind to raise another person. Even our faith will not do it. Our faith will allow Him to move, but it will still always be Him doing it. So, our focus, our confidence and expectation must be in Him and not us. AND, because of that, all the glory and credit go to Jesus not us. Raising the dead is about His name being made great, and people praising Him for His mighty works, not about building a name for ourselves in any way.

Whenever I tried to promote myself with videos, I would find that I would not be able to see the Lord raise the dead. I came to understand that I had to choose between promoting myself and keeping my heart set on the

Lord and making His Name great for His glory and the expansion of His kingdom.

During the years between 2015 and 2019 the Lord allowed me to pray for people to be raised and every time I prayed, I learned more about how to partner with the Lord, hear Him and follow His lead.

In these years, the Lord matured my understanding of how to operate in faith for raising the dead. He showed that it was just not only a matter of keeping my heart focused on Him and having pure motives and not self-centered ones.

In addition, Jesus taught me that if He said He would raise the dead, then He would, but if He did not tell me that He would, then He would not. And remember because I was living and praying for people in India, where people demanded to see proof of God's power and they were likely to beat people who offered false hope. Learning to hear the Lord and wait for Him to tell me when He was going to raise someone, helped my life tremendously.

On January 25th, 2019, we were in a city and were holding a conference that began the following day. That evening, I was in the sanctuary anointing the sanctuary with water and I found myself saying 'tomorrow He is going to raise a dead person.'

The next day on January 26th the meeting had started, and many people came who were sick expecting to be healed. There were many who came into the meeting this way but one woman who came in extremely sick and was sitting near the back fell over dead during the meeting before she could be prayed for. The people sitting around her started praying immediately for her, and checking her pulse, but there was no breath and no heartbeat. The meeting venue was large, and this occurred toward the back of the meeting, so I was not aware that it had happened. After the people around her had prayed and did everything they knew to do they began to pick her up to carry her back to her house.

But just as they were doing this, I was up front praying over the crowd. As I was praying, just like the night before, the Holy Spirit told me and I said aloud 'God is raising a dead person today, that is what God is doing.'

As I prayed this, to the complete astonishment and joy of her friends and family, the dead woman came back to life, easily breathing on her own and finding that the Lord had also healed her of the maladies she had come to the meeting with.

The lady who had been raised stayed for the rest of the conference, sitting happy and healthy for all to see. This one miracle spread throughout the entire meeting place, and it opened the meeting for many more miracles of healing, and everyone rejoiced!

The venue seated 10,000 people and word of God raising the dead woman circulated around the city quickly and the following day people came from all over to see demonstrations of God's miracle working power.

After this crusade, the Lord continued to open doors for us to travel and hold large meetings, in order for His gospel to be preached and demonstrated in many cities in nations. I was excited to see that the Lord's Word to me that He would use me in big things, was beginning to come to pass.

One of the precious testimonies of Jesus' power to raise the dead, happened during this time before the pandemic began and our international travel was suspended. I received a phone call from a set of parents who were pregnant and had been told that their baby had died in the womb. It was their first child. Their first baby boy. They were not only broken-hearted, but they believed God could bring the baby back to life. They had heard that I had seen the Lord raise the dead and so contacted our ministry and asked if I would pray over their baby.

The mother put the phone up to her stomach. When she did, I spoke directly to the little boy 'Hey champion!'

I said boldly and joyfully, 'come back to life! You need to do God's work!' I had immense joy and faith when I prayed for this little one and knew that the Lord had healed him.

The parents were filled with faith as well! They went back to the doctor and asked him to check again for a heartbeat. At first the doctor would not and insisted that he had checked the baby before, knew the baby had died and that there was no reason to check again.

However, the parents insisted and begrudgingly, not wanting to contribute to further emotional harm to the parents, the doctor rather sorrowfully put the stethoscope up to the mother's stomach.

'Whoosh!' with a swift quick, the baby boy inside gave a mighty kick and the stethoscope jumped off the mother's belly!

He was alive and well! More than well! He had indeed come back like I had commanded him to and was ready and raring to go to get his work done for the Lord! And his FIRST work that this little baby accomplished was to give the doctor the biggest SURPRISE in His life and a powerful firsthand testimony of the goodness and power of God! That is quite a ministry the little boy entered, ac-complishing so much even before his mother gave birth to him!

The doctor was overjoyed but stunned and declared that only God could have done such a wonderful miracle for the family! The baby was delivered a few months later, completely healthy, and the parents wrote and sent video to our ministry so we could rejoice with them! God is a good God! And God is a powerful God! And He uses His power on our behalf!

CHAPTER 9:

THE HOLY SPIRIT RISES IN TIMES OF TROUBLE

When the enemy shall come in like a flood,
the Spirit of the Lord shall lift up a standard against him.
Isaiah 59:15

As the pandemic began to unfold in spring of 2020, our ministry, like most others, found we were not able to travel internationally and so once again returned our attention to our home front of India.

Acts 17 says that we are each born at the exact place and time for God's purpose for our lives. And just as God had just walked me through a season of pressing into seeing Him raise the dead, a great need arose in our nation to have the Lord move supernaturally in His miracle power. Like many nations, India's government-imposed quarantines in efforts to slow the spread of the Covid-19 virus through the 1.3 billion people when there was no vaccine and little known about the impact the virus would have on the general population. There was a lot of fear worldwide during the first months of Covid and many people succumbed to sickness or even death out of panic or fear of this unknown disease.

But while tragedy was repeating itself in many households, God had also arranged for our ministry to be returned to India and minister to many of those people in great need. We did not have the ability to gather in large meetings of course, not even small meetings were permitted. But we received many requests to pray for people during those years and were grateful that the Lord was able to use us to help relieve some of the suffering.

During that season we prayed for as many people as the Lord opened doors for us to pray for. The quarantine in our country only allowed people to be out of their homes for no more than 4 hours a day to go and gather food for their family. And yet, during this season, we the Lord was gracious and kind and allowed us to pray for 20 people who had died, and mostly of Covid. Out of the 20 most of them were Christians, and 12 of them came back to life. Praise the Lord! He was still moving in India and in the hearts of His people!

Even a global pandemic was not only not enough to stop God's mighty moving, but He rose up and gave our ministry an increase of opportunity to see Him raise the dead during that season. God always has a people prepared for what is coming ahead. He always has a plan that will turn what the enemy meant for evil into something that will bring blessing to many, even up to many nations. Genesis 50:20.

God continued to guide and bless our ministry to be able to provide food and God's miracle power to many who otherwise would have suffered and been without. He started connecting us to wonderful people all over the globe from Australia to Malaysia to the United States, El Salvador, Mexico, and many other nations where the harvest is ready but the workers are few.

If you have been touched by God's work in my life, I want you to know that God has just as wonderful plans for you. He really does. He is not a respecter of persons. What He will do for one person, He will do for another.

Today as you finish reading this short account of God's supernatural power and His deep concern and love for people from all walks of life, take a moment to talk directly to Him. Tell Him that you make yourself available for Him to move through you with His supernatural power as well. Tell Him that you believe that He is a God of His Word and if He says He has empowered us to lay hands on the sick and see them recover, then you will believe Him and take action on that. Give God your YES. Do not hold back because maybe you have experienced rejection. I did. And the Lord was faithful and healed me and saw me through to the other side.

Do not hold back because maybe you have experienced failure. I did.

I failed many times before I saw one person rise from the dead.

Whether God has placed a desire in you to raise the dead, to heal the sick, build a church, start a business, become an evangelist of missionary, or raise a family of strong believers, know that He is with you, He is for you and He has enough power to pull that desire off and plenty of power left over!

God is a good God! God is a powerful God! God is the God of the supernatural!

May you spend the rest of your days until the Lord returns, passionately seeking Him above all things, and then His beautiful, supernatural plans that He has for you! May you be FILLED to the fullness of His love and His power in Christ Jesus.

1 Cor. 2:4

My message and my preaching were not with wise and persuasive words, but with a demonstration of the Spirit's power

I am not ashamed of the gospel, for it is the power of God unto salvation. Romans 1:16

"Now to Him who is able to do exceedingly abundantly above all that we ask or think, according to the power that works in us, **to Him be glory in the church by Christ Jesus to all generations, forever and ever.** *Amen Eph. 3:20*

In Christ,

Samuel Vardhan

APPENDIXES

How can I be born again?

The Bible teaches us that we were all born innocent, but with something called iniquity in us. Iniquity is the desire to sin or go against the law of love in God. So, at some age without ever having been taught or trained to sin, we all made choices that did not line up with God's character. That is why the Bible says we have all fallen short of the glory of God. Romans 3:23 The wage of sin is death or separation from God.

But because God so loved the world, He sent His own Son Jesus to live a sinless life on our behalf and die to pay the penalty for our sins. He went to Hell for three days and then rose from the dead and sits now at the right hand of God in heaven. He is pulling on you today to receive His life, death, and resurrection, as payment for your sin and for entrance into the kingdom of God. Today is

YOUR day of salvation. The Bible says that when you believe in your heart that Jesus is the Son of God, that He was born of a virgin, and was both man and God, and that is the Lord, then you will be saved. Romans 10:9. All who call on the Name of the Lord, which is Jesus, shall be saved. Romans 10:13

Today, if you understand that you have committed at least one sin, you have done at least one thing wrong, told a lie, been angry and hurt someone's feelings, taken something that was not yours, said something wrong or did something wrong, then you can receive Jesus' free offer of forgiveness. Today, right where you are at, go directly to Him and tell Him 'Jesus, I know I am a sinner and have done at least one thing wrong. I believe that you came from heaven to earth to save and rescue me from my sins. I ask you today to forgive my sins. I ask you to forgive me and ask you to come and live inside of my heart today. I make you the Lord of my life. I want to learn your Word and I want to live a life that is pleasing to you. I thank you that from today forward, you are my Savior, God is my Father and heaven is my home.'

The Bible says that when you have prayed this prayer and asked God to forgive and save you, that He said "YES" and came on the inside with His Holy Spirit. And that you now belong to Him. If you have received Him today, tell someone! And then find a church home to attend that teaches the Bible and how to live the life that God has for you! He has a wonderful life planned for you!

How can I receive God's power in my life?

Baptism of the Holy Spirit

This is an amazing gift Jesus has for you! After you have received Jesus as your savior, the Holy Spirit has now come to live on the inside of you. He will never leave you. Jesus also wants to give you power to walk out the Christian life with great power through the baptism of the Holy Spirit or being filled with the spirit.

Acts 1:8 You will receive power when the Holy Spirit comes upon you.

All of the disciples in the New Testament received this and you can too! There are many benefits the Bible tells us about this gift.

It builds up your spirit, strengthens you on the inside. 1 Cor. 14:4

It is a way to speak/create God's will for you in your life. Romans 8:27

It's a way to receive revelation on the Word of God. 1 Cor. 2:7

It is direct communication with God. 1 Cor. 14:2

It brings spiritual rest and refreshing. Isaiah 28: 11-12

It begins activating spiritual gifts that have been put on the inside of you. Acts 1:8 These are the gifts of tongues, interpretation of tongues, prophecy, gifts of healing, the working of miracles, words of wisdom, words of knowledge and the gift of discernment.

It is a way to praise God. 1 Cor. 14:17

Intimacy with Jesus. John 16:13

How do you know you've received the gift of the Holy Spirit?

While Peter was still speaking these words, the Holy Spirit came on all who heard the message. Those with Peter were astonished that the gift of the Holy Spirit had been poured out even on the Gentiles. For they heard them speaking in tongues and praising God. Acts 10:44-46

So, speaking in tongues is the evidence. How do you start doing this?

Receiving the gift of the Holy Spirit is very easy because it already belongs to you once you've received Jesus as your savior. Speaking is just moving your mouth and having sound come out! Begin to tell the Lord "thank you Lord for this gift" and just start speaking. Because there are so many wonderful benefits that come with this gift, the enemy says the same thing to everyone who receives this gift. So as soon as you start, the first thing your mind will tell you is 'this isn't tongues, this is gibberish.' Well, this thought is not true! The enemy can't help but like that is just who he is. John 8:44 Keep speaking with boldness and the thought will leave and God will confirm to your spirit that this is from Him. Continue to pray in the spirit every day, build this time up. It will bring an increased strength, joy, love for God and others and many other wonderful new things to you! Praise the Lord for His wonderful salvation and gifts! He is greatly to be praised!

How does God speak to people today?

God wants to speak to you and I every day through His Word. His Word is God's Voice speaking to you and me. The Old Testament is written for us, and the New Testament is written TO us. God speaks through His Word and the inner working of His Holy Spirit. He can also speak to us through dreams, visions, audible voice, the gifts of the spirit, five-fold ministers, or other believers or even circumstances. But in any form of communication that He uses, what He says always lines up with His written Word. The more you want to 'hear God speak' or 'give you a Word' of direction, the more you want to be IN His written Word.

What can I do to help myself to hear the Lord better and better?

There are a few concrete actions we can take to allow ourselves to hear the Lord to a great degree of detail and accuracy:

- Be in the Word everyday, reading, studying, meditating the Word

- Pray in the Spirit, using the prayer language of tongues. This strengthens our spiritual ears and eyes and mind to understand the Word and hear the voice of the Lord and prompting of the Holy Spirit.

- Keep your heart right with God. Keep in peace toward the Lord and live in peace with others as much as it depends on yourself.

- Keep out of sin and unforgiveness. Knowingly staying in sin, or harboring unforgiveness will make it harder to hear the voice of the Lord.

- Stay in fellowship with other believers. Do not forsake the assembly of the brethren. Stay in spiritual order and submission to those in spiritual authority over you and in a spirit of unity and bond of peace.

- Obey any revelation you have from the written Word to the best of your ability. If you have a revelation of tithing, then tithe. If you have a revelation of healing, maintain that healing. Walk in obedience to anything the Lord has already shown you in His Word.

- Walk in obedience and take action on anything that the Lord has already told you prophetically.

How can I connect to the ministry of Prophet Samuel Vardhan?

Samuel Vardhan Ministries is an international ministry dedicated to sharing the love of Jesus, the plan of salvation and demonstrating the power of God to the nations. We are based out of India, with headquarters in the United States. We fulfill the great commission by:

- Holding prophetic training schools
- Feeding programs in India
- Free education programs in India and Africa
- International crusades
- Preaching in local churches across the nations

Contact us at: SamuelVardhan.com Info@Samuel-vardhan.com

There are 4 ways you can become active in our ministry:

Pray: Pray that the Lord continues to open up doors of utterance for us to preach the gospel. Prayer for our crusade events, feeding programs and that the Lord continues to send us workers. Need Sam to give us what to pray for.

Attend: Check our website for current traveling itinerary.

Invite: Invite Prophet Samuel to your church, conference or crusade event.

Give: Partner with us to reach the lost for the gospel. You can give securely on our website.